ALL THINGS LOSE THOUSANDS OF TIMES

ANGELA PEÑAREDONDO

Front cover art by Mike Saijo
Back cover art and inside art, "The Invention of Death" and
"King's Birdie" by Sal Lloren
Author photograph by Van Lee, Antonio Coelho Da Silva,
Anton Peñaredondo and Chie Yamada
Book design and layout by Lawrence Eby

Printed and bound in the United States
Distributed by Ingram

Winner of the Regional Hillary Gravendyk Prize, judged by
Chad Sweeney

Published by Inlandia Institute
Riverside, California
www.inlandiainstitute.org
First Edition

ALL THINGS LOSE THOUSANDS OF TIMES

INLANDIA BOOKS
RIVERSIDE, CALIFORNIA

Angela
Peñaredondo

CONTENTS

THREE

FOUR

JUDGE'S STATEMENT

Elastic, dimensional, all-together convincing, Angela Peñaredondo's debut *All Things Lose Thousands of Times* wields the language as a mountain wields a storm, in phrases that pivot, reverse, wander, tighten, leap and fall through geographies of the body, an inward archipelago of experience, individual and collective, all past and flooded, all future and on fire, bearing unflinching witness to courage, revelation and sexuality, to life and to the lives of women where "their mothers have turned into mangroves" and where "her father found us / as I knelt before her, knees / on church-cold tile." A profoundly alert and loving book that sings and celebrates the cosmic interplay of forms. This is what poetry can do. I feel rescued by it.

—Chad Sweeney

FOREWORD

Angela Peñaredondo's *All Things Lose Thousands of Times* is, in reductive terms, an exploration of the transition from wakefulness to sleep traversing origin, methodology, and the limits of human knowledge through point of view and the subconscious, exploiting the chance effects and unexpected juxtapositions of image and syntax. Conjuring Pablo Neruda, Charles Baudelaire, and Marcel Marceau, Peñaredondo's collection of poems seek to mime continental crossings, / *...another playing appears. / The back of a sofa poses as an obstruction / before it converts to a raised stage... / ,* where poet embodies both voyeur and flâneur with intentionality—such careful witnessing:

> *Tomorrow, under this humidity, your skin shall remain the same: a trapping glow, a zinging inside a dangle of light. The grasp of a jaw upon a jaw clicking into place like a small key into a lock. The manic of thighs. The inside of our mouths bruised and tongue, a hidden forager for flesh all sizes—just the same. Arch and pull of what is already broken, the only forgiveness I ask. Let belief be this.*

Reading Peñaredondo's experiments in *All Things Lose Thousands of Times*, I can't help but think of the ways "identity and subjectivity are formed within a net of cultures, not just one," (x) speaking to the truisms of mythos and mettle, those places where

iii

the unexpected peripheral repositions itself. Sites serve as gestures that reach toward "development" and or "civility" as seen through a canonical lens and the complications that arise from spiritual want and the bodily desire of the poet:

> *You think of the different countries now washed*
> *   over by rain,*
> *   very well,*
> *they tell you under fractions of sky,*
> *because they've watched all things lose*
> *thousands and thousands of times.*

Such longing and omission conflates the edges of— everything is connected as bodily boundaries are muddled by notions of return:

> *I didn't go back to reawaken or recover*
> *the relics, nor puzzle*
> *what I'd become...*
> *or ask the particulars of...*
> *When a tree falls, its roots*
> *aim jagged, pointing*
> *in all directions...*

Peñaredondo courts spiritual perplexity in proximity to contemporary discourses grounded in female, brown, queer landscapes where the improvement of the aesthetic appearance occurs through/by the changing of its contours, through the addition and subtraction of ornamental features, / *...altars never wonder... / tell me the incantations for this kind shedding.* Offering a poetic aesthetic that gestures to larger conversations: what is it to be a queer, brown woman dispossessed by a faith whose God refuses you? What is the signature, abutting edge, stitch that destabilizes notions of this construct?

> ...and yes, surprise!
> Even women betray each other
> for contour,
> for beauty,
> for burn again.

How to negotiate the cultural and historical as locus—ions in the air acting as drops of mist refracting light—on these larger questions? *All Things Lose Thousands of Times* bridges poetry and the social/cultural world as a reverberation of neorealist and surrealist points of view, where the materiality of a body, as a context, grows larger than the poet as self. These poems palpitate underneath the personal, familial, national, racial, and notions of gender as a means to formulate a rhetoric, "that celebrates and returns again and again to the invisible space of the pocket, its lint. The viscera of the pouch where the forgotten and the discarded collect..." (93). A language of investigation and sight emerges in Peñaredondo's collection, *only you could scrub clean / but there is no lye / strong enough for this skin.*

—Mg Roberts, Author of *not so, sea* (Durga Press)

References

Myung Mi Kim, "Thirty and Five Books," *Dura* (New York: Nightboat Books, 2008), X.

Mg Roberts. Afterword. *Nests and Strangers: On Asian American Women Poets.* Ed. Timothy Yu. (Berkeley: Kelsey Street Press, 2015), 93.

for Chico
(& for our travels that gathered and parted)

Elongated on the dirt
one skiff is rescued
not by the angelic
but whatever is loose in the waters
                    always seeking death,
                    that little burning thing.

ONE

ANOTHER WORLD GATHERS

I sleep in a bedroom once a horse
stable for a monastery.

The monks have all turned
& the cork trees stripped to red.

I am a weak thing. A body down,
an eaten up mosquito net.

A white candle drives out fear,
a red one drives out lust.

CONCERTO IN F MINOR

There is no spring through window shades
of Hotel Little Regina. Only
the severe bones of Bach's harpsichord.

Mercy falls curiously into the river.
Flesh, a boat swaying as violent

as Bataille's frail body of want,
his naked boy lying on the grass
at night, soaked and saying:

the starry universe,
which merely serves as backdrop.
His bare curve now in mud—and if I prevail

towards dream—will turn to a breached animal.
I see us bedding in these scant leaves.
But you, I don't know.
This yellow earth. The pale clay.

WOMEN AND CHILDREN FOR SALE

1

So young   like silk heaven!
Light pulls my bamboo   hard (aaahs and ooohs)
    for this sweet potato!
Forget her   and the yellow
    shutters.
        Bicycles swarm—
        they're coming.

2

        Broiled-fish-Asian landscape   where
    mercenaries
first hoisted   their grandiose operas,
        tossed   their nets out for
                                translucent shrimp!
Jet a marriage,   carry her to bed,
        calmly jaywalk
                        with confidence.

3

        The domestic market:
he's paying all   before a thousand selected   queens
saddled behind glass and stage.   They're wearing
    the tightest lace
    & blue jeans.
            Miss, this is something!
            Obsession,   a little job abroad.

4

They shake,
      smoldering before gilded midnight.
      They come   primed for   EXPLOSION.
One applauds,   frozen-faced
at Franz Bar in Alaminos.   Her name   Ka Rene.

5

Before we go any further,
        let me tell you why I seek struggle:
    a little noodle soup and
    rice liquor,
    the debris   of a giant   firecracker,
        to plunge from a butterfly
            of a boat on golden waters.

6

    Good Mor-Ning,
 North America!
Hell-O.
I boil the classics, roast with plum sauce
   and the fiercest ginger.
I eat *Gone with the Wind.*
     Scarlet exists in the Bay of Tonkin.
           It was difficult to get a visa.

7

Demon faith carries a girl
       over fields   over Red River—
      pagodas in full smoke.
    Altars never wonder.
Flower balloons arrive

from the village, interspersed
in small powder loads.   Eyes, alive!

8
If you go out early, good-looking!
                The damp winds   bear the image
                                half a world away
arranged before children were beaten.
                We're in the tropics,
                above sea level   at the latitude of Calcutta,
Indochina.   Bombs   farms   annexations.
The northern border flouts. They suggest   that I
      don't need a translator.

9
Take the train across Cambodia, very rich people!

        Good food,
        baskets on strings,
        bikinis front row,
        mandarin robes,
        blue bodhisattvas,
        gold, more children.

I ask a young man,
Care how they look?
Looks chaotic, but paved over,
they're gone without a trace.

10
Go away   crackling fry of beef,
        butchering of two dogs   for the pot

                                                    of love.
Been bone-hungry   three days,   another waxes
     and I can hardly move.
           Private resistance
                of the bloodstream.

                              11
An inscription on a drum:
           water buffalo
                and pig.
           A dragon inside
                wherever I go.

AUBADE CASSETTE

I sew together pieces with string
from 77 Poems, the white
page widely open, Lacerda says,
nakedness is more and more terrible.

Each diagonal of loss is measured:
a running field, a perimeter
of mouth, each crawl to rumpled sleep.
But to loss Darling, I prefer talk
until the flags and meat burn.
I replay it in my head like Hikmet's
smoldering red chimneys of Istanbul
and bars of Bursa and yes, surprise!
Even women betray each other
for contour,
for beauty,
for burn again.

But the disorderly placement of hands,
the barrier made from the vertical of cigarette
against chin meant a diagram
of secrets and I am tired of the startling.
The clear plain of desertion.

BLACK TIGERS

*A bunch of breasts from either arm, and that
lone question—do you friend, even now, know
what it is all about?*
   —Wole Soyinka, from "Civilian and Soldier"

The sun slips between panels of fichus. Dripping.
 She travels only at night. Beds in ditches for too
 many hot nights.

Her body arrives in the ghoulish thicket
 like so many girls do with a bomb strapped
 between both breasts.

*

The Velcro harness starts as an itchy burn then
 turns into second skin. Black tape travels like
 zebra stripes. Tar.

 Her thumping chest—an only blanket.

*

A rigorous comb and cut with unsharpened shears.
 See how girls shape up real well, ready to
 scatter the ground any time.

Litter across the jungle, turn a city to shambles.
 Shoulder, breast, elbow, lip no longer shackled.
 They tie their buns back

in bundles and bundles of black. Their mothers
 have turned into mangroves. No, a dream and

an ochre river. The men form into a line under
shadows of strangler figs.

*

The wild bird's plucked and severed with ease.
 Plumes and pink meat in her hands. Gummed
 to dips of fingers.

Teeth like sun, like the scaled peel of snake fruit.
 But when she's strapped, how she can slither
 through any damn hole, any dark line

of in-between. *For country,* she says, *I shall be
 severed.* Spread with voracity, then refined to
 seeds and meat. This land. All hunger, girls.

*

The manioc and mud and rust mud of a river.
 What a mud muddy soldier she's become.
 Breasts fastened mounds underneath fatigues

and sweat. A topaz sari disposed of on that river's
 shore. It's lined in reeds needling moisture.
 Mosquitos pepper running water.

*

The buzz, buzz and zip. Inevitable sting of cyanide,
 then a smooth leg the hue of dunes and cherry
 bark. An ornament, a trophy, all alone lying
 there—full gleam.

EVE'S MISTRESS

We long indulged in a cave as grass

does half-awake and shaking morning.

We let the scene unpeel us like rogues.

Only the lilies knew beyond the rogue's

exterior that we laid out like grass

delicately silver each morning.

The mole on her leg marks a day's morning,

but he exorcised us with his rogues,

saints they were not. Inside the tall grass,

their sharp spines, quivering knives of rogues.

WOMAN LEAVES
PSYCOANALYST OFFICE

Oil on Canvas, *Mujer Saliendo Del Psicoanalista*
by Remedios Varo

My eyes can do nothing else
but stare at the way she grips

her father's beard
  as she leaves the office.
                    His head a sliver of meat

hooked between
her thumb and pointer finger.

*

So many women I know have it hard letting go.
The first woman I fell in love with,

all my fear inside my head.
Rainwater funneling down a drain.

When she turned around,
  the back of her neck
                    no longer a neck
                    but an extension of my arm.

*

She holds him precarious,
                    a savory chicken heart, un-skewered
over a swollen, hankering tongue.

I think what unabashed courage.
What backbone of natural sorcery is this?

Tell me the incantations
for this kind shedding.

*

Why I wanted her or wanted to be her.
How I hated her.

When she snipped off all her locks,
let them blazon on the bathroom floor.

Her father found us
as I knelt before her,
  knees kissing
            on the church-cold tile.
            His glare pale as carabao bone.

His fist, that year's watershed.

*

She suspends
        her father's head.

A dead goldfish before a toilet bowl.
If I look long enough, I can almost hear
                                flush.

BEFORE ENCOUNTERING THE INABANGA RIVER

It is an unnamed bridge like a kind but unbearable
light that walks through walls.
Do you ever see them?
        Those ever-impatient

bobbing towards the flawed flame,
over and over cities
and the spout of fountains.

I want to be that kind
who can walk through a wall of fifty lives
like river, wet dirt,
its wild aloe
prodding the mustard grass.
Every confession now under water.

Shadows, be not the only thing
living in the strapped, barred up,
padlocked doors
of a gypsy church.

To rope, arm, thigh, white
       neem, stars. God
       lets me go.
Why they even come back,
those spoiled stars.
I can't know.

I'd rather be whoever bathes
in the monsoon, knees swaying—
unequaled. Wanting   allows gospel.

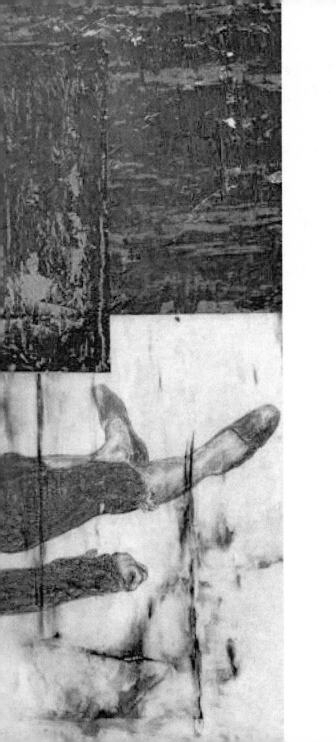

TWO

THE YOUNG

Chatterbox / of a slow boy / a thing / a toy
May he / have life / like an unfallen tree
What if / lush life / sounded / young / monk / savoy

and bruised arms / became trumpets / enrapt joy
What god / if I god / let me / be more than she
Chatterbox / of a slow boy / some thing / some toy

Frantic for love / in dark clubs / what fine boys
think I've seen you / carried down to the sea
What if lush / life sounded / young monk savoy

and days always / tasted that good / agree
like the rubber / bends / elasticity
Chatterbox / of a slow boy / thing thing / toy toy

Next time / those knuckles fly / hit redeploy
Dance some / even when city burns / times three
What / if lush life / sounded young / monk savoy

Through ash / broke glass / Venus is viceroy
Who can tell its weight / when reflex / joy's small knee
Chatterbox of a slow boy / I thing / I toy
What a life / lush sounded / young monk / savoy

THE ISLANDER MOTEL

*Many years ago—how many? I have no idea; all this goes
back into the mists...*

—Charles Baudelaire
from "The Philosophy of Toys"

It starts with the ones who pay by the hour.
A silent street and a mask hung down to her feet.

Enters a face that goes white like the bathroom's
    everything.
In the diminished room, she seeks to taste giving
    hands.

How they hold marvelously everything.
Here, eyes separate into pennies of joy

tossed over sheets clotted with azaleas. She can feel
her smell, her own opening and closing like a robe.

Once in the divide, another playing appears.
The back of a sofa poses as an obstruction
before it converts to a raised stage.

Shake the lights up. Her figure,
a-much-of-nothing-machine with parts that buzz,
illuminating after remedy.

Offerings seized: uncanny shapes   knuckle in
    a mouth   foot nestled in a fold.

Exits a stunted bug with trembling legs. The spells
    separate
what is left of her muted gleam.

IN DELAY
WITH MARCEL MARCEAU

It all happens in suspension.
        A kite let loose.
I give up.   *I'm flying,*
I give up, each hand,
a waving siren, says.

To command the invisible
imperfectly moving
is to inhale their hovering pain.
Like a confection to your nose:
        a thread   a knot
        a tear   a dice roll.

Inside your throat, captured
in equidistance, laughter
        accumulates and dies.

The ground weighs nothing but clouds
and your face, nothing, too.
But where are the freed
sparrows that come to you?

Are you one extremity dancing
 from each separation of the body?
        Your arm fights off spring,
        lengthens into a tightrope.

You fight with yourself and the animals.
You fight with John the Baptist

at the flats of the Jordan,
fight the saints wielding their scripts

until your mouth toothless
and mulled black.
        You look   gone as a boat
        in direction of some heaven.

WHAT SHE WILLS
[THE TREES BEHIND]

With all the danger involved
at least you know the missing
is not a blank letter or diminished
garden, instead your mouth full
of such shattering sea
and the peninsulas ravaged
like the lean flesh of a neck.
                              How many times
barefoot and without map, you must
have told God through the slim crevasse
of both palms, you were ready
to let go of all that water.

The wax-like geography of a province
and grandmother finally buried
in Laguna, its quiet shrine
as close to infinity as a small

                         planet gleaming.
Each summer you take what little
money to escape, eager
for the pulpy bits of yourself
moving, no longer cut in half
but some bandaged organism
with each opening of dark

                         an easy
compartment without clinging rope
or barricade, not any exotic brand
or objet trouvé like Laurencin's dancers
rather from clouds an animal forms,
a wild cat slipping inside an oblong hole.

You think of the different countries
now washed over by rain,
                    very well,
they tell you under fractions of sky,
because they've watched all things lose
thousands and thousands of times.

TO DREAM OF DROWNING

Promised down
to a tunneling black.
Of what might be

the opening
of an oversized
body. A god

inside out, tossed
across chasms.

Tissue equals naught.
Throat equals portal.

Because in iron,
the roundedness
and control
of clay, perhaps

this is why I
believe it happens,
this craving

for fierce
locomotion.
For everything Elysian:

funneling
& dark matter
for so long.

When it's done,
a glistening twine

of hair is all
that's left.
Umbilical

from the trident
body to this wrinkled

surface. A dorsal ripples
through the water's
curl. When I wake,

let light be soluble.
Be more than flesh

or pulp. Let me
call it a name

other than sun,
other than another

numb porcelain
taking the hot liquid
after its been sieved.

WOMAN EATS MILKFISH AND HIBISCUS

Long, silvered fatness
she picks out from two hundred bones.

A dream of culling
feathers from a bird wing.

This hunger for the galactic
camouflaged within the leather
of tamarind trees.

This must be her last dinner
with the mga tokó lizards,

with the Visayan islets rusting
and breathing, where seawater
meets corrugated metal.

In the hut next door,
someone's twitchy Sanyo purrs.

Across a garden of bitter
melon, the radio:

Move over
and give us some room.

Through humid foliage, ghosts
never lose their want

for good crooning no matter
the fission or diodes.

Among the reptile's cockled jaws
—she's a hideaway girl.

And with her too, they wait
with their jellied feelers wriggling

to corners of a porch
like unfettered dress straps.

She sponge bathes white fish
in cane vinegar until it umbers,

salts some more before
the declaration of tongue.

When all the flesh is swallowed,
save the flowers for last.

LOVE DARTS

It's 6 p.m., everyone's unpinning laundry from a line—
socks and chemises hovering like assorted doves
while the garbage underneath presides over
the alleys that remorsefully think back.
Maybe it's time to move?
Find a foreign place, sleep with a stranger?

We eat snails and you tell me you're tired of living
    straight:
the bedroom window verging onto a shred of beach,
the morning of eggs with their unbroken
yolks and exposed jelly, the wife
unanswered too many times.

Our waitress drops forks a third time as she holds
a plate of shells piled into a steamy hillock.
I use a toothpick to yank the shriveled larva out.
It springs back into a curl as if hatched

from a deep sea conch like from Paula Rego's *Unicorn*
minus the unicorn and pink dress.
Defensive, you quote Sappho with much resolution,
mention Samuel Delaney.

They've got street credibility. Sure, Spartans
were doing everyone, too. I agree.
Thought it was healthy as vitamins.
Try the clams. They taste less of forests,
gurgling in their translucent stew.

Take it as an act of chivalry. Like cocktail parties

when one goes alone. You don't need to understand
what guests say. You can switch records when no
    one's looking.

Have you heard of blue polymita snails? Their lapis
bodies cooling inside wayside caves, gliding like
    sailors
in their navy suits. No hands. Make love by stabbing.

VAMPIRE IN A BAD CITY

Secrets can be taken apart
like little screws from a dead clock.
She doubts the ancients, rebukes
God-given things, their quick
unnatural handling of power.

Even now, her resistance of the invasions
and their talents: those old furnaces,
houses like lines of jars, fumes bottled
for safekeeping. Tell me
what is even worth keeping.

Without necessity to run, she occupies
corners elsewhere, ascending not
to sainthood but to a being that finally
rewards failure with gifts.

Through her, truth is not a scab but a veil,
lace-less, unfurling itself
into a black wave.

PARTS OF A BODY BEFORE
IT WAS THE BODY'S PAIN

along its sides, the sacrum holds one
thousand petroglyphs but between spine and hill

too much silica and feldspar barring
an opaline valley
its sheet after sheet

taken up by grist
each stringy muscle or marl into another life

the fibula is a palm blade
severed from its length
by monsoon & the mangrove's octopus root

before those brown vestiges of ancient
feasting on cutthroat trout

drinking from the same cave-lake
at the cliff shore
drawdown, the stones say

from above, one is seeing
what is first gathered

then disassembled on the floor
that spirals to summation:

a husk
a crystalline pictograph
a coating of the eyes
once sang of purges:
pearls, pearls, pearls

The confusion lay in a deeper, more secret place...
She has other memories too that she has no right to have.

—Arundhati Roy
from *The God of Small Things*

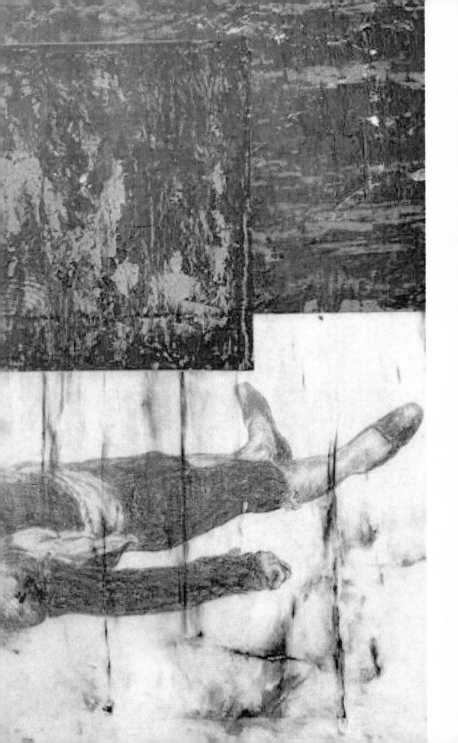

THREE

SITUATION SCULPTURE

To know of the trapped light
inside your head that leads you
to enter one room after another
is to chip away till it shatters
the hard plaster of a culture's
      ribbed mold.

To know the light that comes
is to save a one-wingéd bird,
not one of any blown glass or tinted porcelain
but bird who isn't repelled by thorns,
bird who takes to elm sap without appellation,

thorns that live along the edges,
the very edges of a leaf's veins
know too well the wounded head.

But if the head faithfully allows
the coming light, then it will find
ghostly laundry swaying and without wind
or proof of love or property; so you
must chip away the plastered ribs.

To its killing, who comes closer?
Its instinctive know-how
like culling meat from marrow.
Once, I saw a dotted kestrel perched staunchly
on a red beam, grappling
a headless field mouse;

then a young woman I saw pull out flesh
as if it was a captive piece from her deep
and beyond the clenched doors, the perfume
      of starved, yellow flowers.

THIS BODY MAKES LIGHT

Her body ran like a wind you spoke of,
as if a greyhound was set loose in the desert.

People left her at a Texaco,
dead center of a parched afternoon.

Nothing in her. Only held by bowstring.
I hear your voice, the break

of ribcage lined in silver.
Your story, a love story: an angel

came then left for dead
if there's such a thing.

I say she must have shimmered
like a gunnysack filled

with silver fish bones.
She was an angel you say.

Yes, an unfettered gunnysack,
black moons for eyes.

WHEN WE STOP RUNNING

Away dark curve. Whatever happened? It has no name. These thin stairway walls, this corridor. How they know fever and the red, sad charm of dissipation. Without a ripple of sky. Night comes overdue. And there is no rum or suave to this linen. No need for first nights or homage to them.

Tomorrow, under this humidity, your skin shall remain the same: a trapping glow, a zinging inside a dangle of light. The grasp of a jaw upon a jaw clicking into place like a small key into a lock. The manic of thighs. The inside of our mouths bruised and tongue, a hidden forager for flesh all sizes—just the same. Arch and pull of what is already broken, the only forgiveness I ask. Let belief be this.

In Santiago de Cuba, I remember how it did not rain for days. But hard you drank from me as if I could make it. And I believed that corridor would burst. Each taste of silver necessary, each hard angle inside each dip and ache. Dirt uprooted by the tremor from the apples of your knees. From what nature lives in this place.

THE WORD *REALITY* MEANT NOTHING TO HER

Looking back,
a few friends & nowhere to go,

you watch bodies in carousal,
their chartreuse painted toes spinning
and mottling the earth.

Try different positions.
Stretch outward the range
              of an arrow's shaft.

Legs and ass,
an unbending rose tree—

remember this is a game.
And you slip again as blood does
on ivory silk.

       Now if only you could scrub clean
but there is no lye
strong enough for this skin.

No needles swift nor
deft enough
to allow you to forget.

THIS QUIET RAUCOUS BEFORE STARS

And the train uncoils
city vertebrae in a blinking
strip of light—a postcard of an old face.

On some vista point, sorrel rooftops
and below, nightclubs in red dresses
while vaudeville busboys walk

the lime boulevard.
4 a.m. and no one else
to tell me otherwise, views turn
in slow tempo.
As long as you want me,
I'll stay.

*

A Chesterfield burns a slow crawl
between my knuckles.
Over the colonnade,

my head elevates.
Who am I this time? I say
to a clumsy stack of chairs,
to a cat watching from leaves.

*

A deaf woman laughs in sign language.
Her fingers bouncing on an invisible trumpet.

I don't want anything else,
so come before these hands get cold,
and my torso turns to folded skin.

*

When I was eight, I was an unsmiling ballerina.
The yellow of my costume flared
like a mouth, tiny and celebrated.

Mother clipped a plastic goldfinch
to my hair. On the stage floor, my gloved
feet floated over an X marked in chalk.

And I wondered if grandfather could see me,
his Casanova pin-stripe suit,
elegant and debonair among the spine
of aisles, still here and left again.

*

Love, during that ungodly hour,
I want you to answer in cadenza
like Armstrong's "West End Blues."
Like Bausch's dancers parading
through rain and reverb,
the lightning just before
or like Yusef Lateef's "Yesterdays."

But the instructor utters,
(hard note) *this is how you do it—*
now walk in a straight line—

GIRL MEETS GIRL

Eternity opens with the dark back
of a jazz pianist hunched inside himself.
Girl, with your chipped tooth, distressed shoes,
dark hair that reminds me of Florence,
I speak cotton-soft to my broken heart, now
a vegetable for the dead. So I make
my move, espionage behind champagne
flutes and *clink* of cocktail glasses.
In bathrooms, I know couples moan, finger
each other, déjà vu trapped within tiled
walls. Telepathy is a dirty habit.
After all, night is the *come-what-may*
we all want to be. Night-time is kissing
to dirty movies that echo starlight.
Night means obscenities under
a freeway, without complaint,
our last far-out trip. Companionless,

your hands press upon
the black hole jukebox.

SCRIM

I sit in an old Avenida theatre
called Riviera or Zarah's Clover.
In a fully air-conditioned room
& Amalia Fuentes' fermented velvet,

mahogany seats loosen
into a saline lake.
And when lights dim down to gloss,
I can't move, don't want to.

On the movie screen, faces constellate.
An heiress sculpts her hair
into identical black pearls.

Behind slope of shoulders, a man,
all eyes and ridged brow, writes
with fountain pen over crisp stationary—
a beaming heliograph.

Is it too late to imagine the slow undoing
of buttons? The afternoon dappling
onto a sofa, a passageway
through napping bodies.

Evacuation far from their minds,
unafraid of the beeping sound of failure.
The film continues still.
What elegance now?
        I travel for days.

In the next seat, the faint tang
of washed skin and as if to speak my name,
another man's head turns.

Another unpolished mirror.
Like the dream I've had again & again.
Hands cup my own
          but they embrace only foam.

AS ONE OF EGON SCHIELE'S NUDES

From a tuber moth disrobed, you emerge
and underneath a hungry skeleton.
From your limbs:

> a crumpled sheath of papyrus.
> And your genitals flushed
> to a liturgy of shrunken pulp.

How you savor sacrifice,
appease to swift pierces
like St. Sebastian, wrists bonded

towards the sky. Those nimble arrows,
his face brimming to ambrosia.

> Like him, you recline
> and twist until each

of your fingers like tributaries
angle & spread from the main river.

SMALL PRAYER
FOR UNSATISFIED FEMMES

Forgive her sanity gap,
her credo rattled and thrown down.
Beyond those unnamed hills,
music gone and un-shimmering.

Do not cast her into the rapids
of a twisty river, rupturing
with silken brawl.
For she is both the wrangle
and the salmon. Feathered gills
sucking the salt for air.

Intellect turns violent if tamed.
Think of horses banging
their hooves on the grease
and rust of anything metal.

Do not imprison her behind glass
or sterling—the ordinary pin-up show.
Sweaty coins equal
nothing to this earth.

Forgive her complex reach, groping
to the root. Her basin, once
a halved moon. Hands,
starlings and when open
become a holy book.

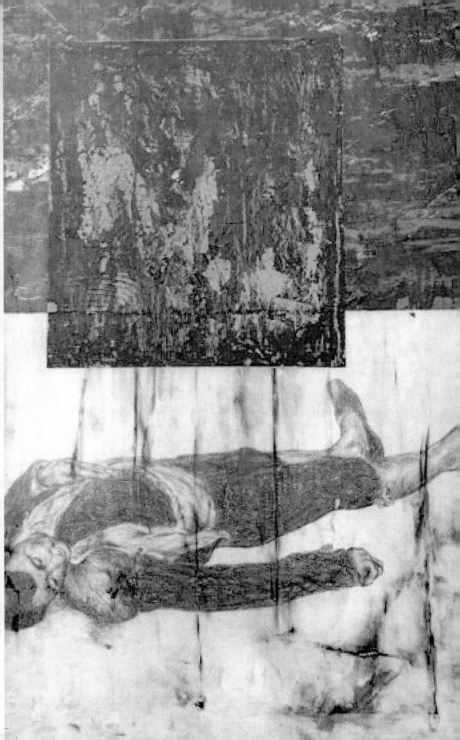

FOUR

BLUES FOR LOVER IN WINTER

I gnaw on dried figs like heart pills
while beyond my balcony, purple prowls
the flanks of sky.

To listen to "Push the Sky Away"
makes my insides shovel
all the heavy lifting. So I say:

Sky, you be good. Don't you leave
even when eyes sling low
into its flesh hearth.
When tongues gouge
as they please, pocket an opening

of both shell and flame. Wasn't it just days ago,
your mouth like butter, our sundry heads sprawled
as far as the colorless hum of sleep.
Still you had to let this good thing throw down.

Stone against stump. To think I thought the arch
of your chin—superlative.
You, kink of a broken radio.

If I could bulldoze you to a slither,
hammer down roads in an old car.
Tat-tat-tat with teeth and tobacco.

Give me ceremony in the thinning mountains
and rifled pines. Silence perches
on the back ledge of your throat.

I become uncovered and it's December.
My head gapes open. The sky
is a giant full of holes.

HE WHO KNOWS
VIOLENCE IS A PRIVILEGE

Assemblage/Box Construction, *L'Humeur Vagabonde*
by Joseph Cornell

There's no room for savagery here:
wild hands on glass cutting
diagonal on an open palm.

His enclosure of seduction like charmed
birds nesting in an aviary.
The un-shattered mouth of youth,

all conserved and bottled:
pieces of wet beach, the only black
star, letters pressed into an amulet.

Through his shadow box, I want
to reconstitute myself,
restore what was not enough.

MEDITATIONS FLOATING ABOVE SINK WATER

Does the secret to great art lie between devotion
and selflessness but with the radio
at Strauss's Four Last Songs
you ask but what of sabotage
the other irrevocable
lined up and hung

why this altar of refuse décor
like a pact made from tin cans and collapsed bottles
belonging elsewhere your head soiled
stuck somewhere in the cosmos
of someone you'll never see again
how you ask for more with praying hands

for a woman
for composure
serenity of islands or maybe
just settling for the melody of trains
skimming beside the Yuba
or hills lush and racing too

in the kitchen bananas
onions and sack of coffee
you wipe down the table with a headscarf
and your mother's cake
never made
the instrumental oil
the boiling raw
and wintry bread

a holding pattern multiplies
you listen all day to its scalding
hello it's avidity

can you remember any invocation
without milk or honey of sex
just a salvaged sun across another juncture

THIS IS WHY I NEED A GODDESS

      I love
those dead-eyed
winos, picking up empties,
their laughter of firework.

The city's full and nuts
but I can't hear
its usual neon,
thrum of its barges.

No, it's quiet
and the devil blinks,
imagines small,
invisible things.

Tonight hurts. Fights.
Drops. Sleeps. It's 3 am—
the Atlantic midnight
for a poet.

Come on, cruel finger
with your cruel
and refusing shake.

Come to me, finger
and not the bottle.
Go paint the bulge on this white
page. Write about hell
factories and cemeteries,

how they dance blurry
pieces of flames.

But instead you give me
the sea. My feet.
You throw love out
like an old sack.

A loaded mouth grinning,
a downer for dead
and night's ripeness
inching toward wreckage.

See, he's got you too.
Finger, fix it and make it right.
Like a seeing-eye dog,
the lord will see you good.

ADVICE FOR TUMBLING OUT OF A RACING CAR

1. Give an offering of smoke to the clavicle, the double-sided arrow of the body. It will tell you which way to swerve.

2. Choose a thunderbird for its three red eyes.

3. Attack like a hawk or guinea fowl. Your opponent: only dove.

4. Before flight, be prepared to roll the torso into an isopod.

5. Tuck chin into chest. You will not swallow dirt. Swallow yourself.

6. You're a stuntwoman. Code name: Èlastique Sauvage.

7. Beauty—not an option.

8. Remember the heart is a miniature bombardier.

9. Do not mistake your legs for bayonets. Use them as catapults.

10. You must and shall be an expert in hinging.

11. Blood will be the first and last thing you see.

12. In this game of chicken, heaven comes after collision.

SELF-PORTRAIT AS MOLLUSCS

They feed on bivulvia in an emergency kind of way.
Their shells snap as two hardened fans—
Because of our likeness
I am jealous.

And their meat ribbons seal and close.
Ancient as Phoenician sea-silk,
transparent genitalia.

So far from a paper napkin or rescued teeth,
their fossils scrape
the stones. I've etched down

this same way before—
splitting savored
under a tongue-less mouth.

And if you want love
and your hand on something
like a ripened thigh,
you must double yourself.
And who doesn't like that?

RETURN

I didn't go back to reawaken or recover
the relics, nor puzzle
what I'd become if left behind.
I did not grow old
with the banyan's hollows
or pray soft to them
before pissing on their leaves.

Sometimes I wish them gone
as if I were floating a thousand
feet off the ground. The haunting
of sexless ghosts
when I was child of broken
bridges & metal fences
outlining this portrait of birth.

I came back not to regret
or ask the particulars of why I left.
When a tree falls, its roots
aim jagged, pointing
in all directions

like a chapel buried up
by the sea, hiding from any
marriage of light. Her cross
poking out of waves
covered in nothing
but a green flesh.

SPIRITS HATE TO BE ALONE

In burned sugarcane fields, the night's ghost
of a sakada farmer in his brimless
hat. Swing of a stale blade
    against moonlight.   I watch the dead.

They love long hours of blackout.
They love this snuffed out match
of a little city.   To the dust that separates

stained lace. To the poor
thrum of humidity.

From the grotto of Saint Lorenzo,
his palm   an offering of birds
turns a sky from its yellow.

On a Milo can, I hear my own mouth.
Suction on a sugar-apple—
    soft, white, meat,
    black, tough, seeds,
between teeth like marbles.

Uncle, light a Flor de Isabela.
In the moment of rising smoke:

crest of a mottled white horse,
the lope on Gimbal's rocky sands,

a girl recognizes the intrusive
pervading like mustard's thick oil.

It's hunger too.
The way of salt & rain
eating tin.

TOWARDS FLESH

Corroding the stone and with it too. Water. The water cutting the wreck with each intricate of downpour. And so the ground goes devoutly to mud. We muddied ships. From China to Cebu to the red beams of San Juanico. From the sticky low tide of a shore. We want you to want to pray for us. We like the refrain. We lie down in the salt, marooned with only our mouths: only the web of wetness, what we want has been written out. Across the hulk of it all, we want the sky to want us too. And for what sky there is inside us to be devout.

A PRIMITIVE TOY

And with loneliness reaches maturity,
a kind of god says so.
    See her name as she is known:

stout leather, oblivious with a torso
too tight and a neck   too loose
and everything for her exists
    in her recumbence.

I imagine she dreams
of being elephantine
thus would raise the trunk
    she does not have

and not come back to the ground
because it meant the possibility
of being mounted   or of being crippled
    by a young bull.

With inclination to surrender
so massive a body, a barge   the bulk
    collapsing before a water hole.

WHEN THE SAINTS TURNED
TO CARNIVAL DANCERS

like glistening trinkets   fired over the new world
they throw themselves   as if shot from rifles   shower
of dawn's confetti   the seawalls   the shanties
swivel in alignment   for their divine legs   curved
unbreakable cocoons   floated up by lilies &
knavish anthuriums   all perfumed   bellies oiled of rain
of palm juice   a renegade waltz   pull & wrestle of wings
pelvises bound by glitz   little strings   no one will care   no one
will remember what they did   or who
they kissed   what they drank   touched or blessed
cup of holy   the last warm mouth
a lover's rival   shot   in a dance against the wall
necks unrolled   upward   not for the father   but for flesh, style &
a garrison of stars   knowing too well   ecstasy cushions any fall
their cloths of celebration   discarded   then trampled upon   like fallen enemies
without their charms   unchained on the sand   do you know
that a swarthy pepper   expels   even when the finale withers
to a peel   when the fierce regalia   shed
for one night as far   as our puny   memories can ride   they return
to part-time animals   at last   submitting
what is left—   beauty at our bare feet

NOTES

In the poem, "Concerto in F Minor," the quote, *the starry universe, which merely serves as backdrop* is from Georges Bataille's "Story of an Eye." The title of this poem is from Johann Sebastian Bach's composition, Concerto No.5 in F Minor (Largo).

In "Aubade Cassette," the quote: *nakedness is more and more terrible* is from an Alberto Lacerdo poem from his poetry collection, *77 Poems*.

"Eve's Mistress" is written as a tritina.

"Before Encountering the Inabanga River": The Inabanga River is the largest river on the island of Bohol in the Philippines. A bridge called the Friendship Bridge (17.5 kilometer bridge) was in the process of being built when this poem was written. This bridge was said to provide transportation access between the islands of Cebu and Bohol. It is said that Cebu needs Bohol's water supply from the Inabanga River and Bohol is in need of Cebu's excess power.

"Woman Eats Milkfish and Hibiscus" borrows the lyrics, *move over and give us some room* from the song, "Glory Box" by Portishead.

"Love Darts": Paula Rego is a contemporary Portuguese visual artist. Paula Rego's *Unicorn* is a lithograph that depicts two women in pink dresses and a hobby stick unicorn toy.

"Vampire in a Bad City" is after the 2014 film, *A Girl Walks Home Alone At Night*, directed by Ana Lily Amirpour.

"Situation Sculpture" is written as a nonce that borrows and alters the form from Pablo Neruda's poem, "If Destruction Merges with Light."

The title of the poem, "The Word *Reality* Meant Nothing to Her" is a phrase from Clarice Lispector's *Hour of the Star*.

In "Scrim," the Avenida theatre makes reference to the art deco theaters of Manila, where vaudeville performances took place before the screening of movies. Amalia Fuentes is a famous Filipina actress from the 1950s.

"This is Why I Need a Goddess": This title is attributed to the second and third line of Jack Spicer's poem, *Any fool can get into an ocean/but it takes a goddess/to get out of one.*

"Blues for Lover in Winter": "Push the Sky Away" is a song by Nick Cave and the Bad Seeds.

In, "Spirits Hate to be Alone," sakada farmers are Filipino plantation laborers who work or have worked in the sugar cane fields of Hawaii or the Philippines (mainly the Visayas region).

"Return" borrows its title from Alberto Lacerdo's poem "Return" as well as attributes its form to his poem.

In "Towards Flesh," the San Juanico is a Pan-Philippines Highway that connects Tacloban (Leyte) to Santa Rita (Samar). This poem is dedicated to both the living and the dead after Typhoon Haiyan/Yolanda.

ACKNOWLEDGEMENTS

I am eternally grateful to my father (Andres Peñaredondo), mother (Ivonne Peñaredondo) and brother (Anton Peñaredondo) for their love, support, and prayers. I thank them for their appreciation for stories and movies. These elements will always be a part of my creative life.

Big thank you to Katie Ford for her dedication and discipline in the sharpening of this book's vision and voice. To Allison Benis White for her unmatched openness, guidance and spark. To Michael Jayme for enlightening me with his eloquence and his astute appreciation for the details and inner yearnings of a story and a poem. Super kudos to the Maestro of Poetic Fluxus as well as artistic divination, cosmic channeling and transnational community, Juan Felipe Herrera. There is no one like him. To Allison Adele Hedge Coke for her strength, wisdom and constant presence as a true mentor and friend. To the dangerously talented Ronaldo Wilson and Carmen Giménez Smith; their art inspires me to move unapologetically beyond. To the amazing mentors and poets who read these poems and shared their knowledge in some shape or form: Fred Moten, Patricia Smith, Mary Ruefle, my workshop colleagues at UC Riverside, VONA and Tin House.

To the Convento do Mértola artist-in-residence program for providing a unique space for creative incubation. To the University of California, Riverside's MFA Program in Creative Writing and

Writing for the Performing Arts and The University of California Institute for Research in the Arts for their support. To the Tin House Summer Writing Workshop and Dzanc Books' Disquiet International Literary Program for providing support and community.

Endless thanks to the talented artist, Mike Saijo for being both a generous and prolific collaborator on the cover and text art (original font name: refugee camp). To Sal Lloren for allowing me to incorporate his artwork as an added and deeper extension to this book. To Melissa Sipin-Gabon for her warm and generous counsel. To Mg Roberts for sharing with me parallel poetic vision, insight and camaraderie. To Antonio Coelho Da Silva for his unwavering support and faith throughout my time at UCR. Stars and lights to Patima Komolamit and Steve Roy for their unflappable friendship and belief in all my layers. To Brian Stephens for the hearty exchange of love & intellect, and for being my comrade on many levels.

Many thanks to the wonderful writers of Inlandia Institute: Cati Porter, Lawrence Eby and Chad Sweeney.

CREDITS

Grateful acknowledgement is made to the editors of the print and online journals in which some of the poems, sometimes as different versions, appeared or are forthcoming:

"Vampire in a Bad City" has appeared in *Dis·Articulations*, a collaborative poetry project by Terry Wolverton. "Black Tigers" has appeared in the *South Dakota Review.* "Woman Eats Milkfish and Hibiscus" has appeared in *Kore Press.* "Girl Meets Girl" has appeared in *Thrush Poetry Journal.* "Women and Children for Sale" and "Spirits Hate to be Alone" have appeared in *The Margins*, a part of the Asian American Writers' Workshop. "Love Darts" has appeared in *Cream City Review.* "This Quiet Raucous Before Stars" appeared in *Reservoir Journal.*

"Parts of a Body before It Was the Body's Pain" will appear in the *Berkeley Poetry Review.* "Towards Flesh" will appear in *Southern Humanities Review.* "Advice for Tumbling Out of a Racing Car" will appear in *Tuesday; An Art Project.* "Before Encountering the Inabanga River," "When the Saints Turned to Carnival Dancers" and "Vampire in a Bad City" will appear in *Tayo Literary Magazine.* "Concerto in F Minor," "What She Wills [The Trees Behind]" and "Woman Leaves Psychoanalyst Office" will appear in *Twelfth House Literary Journal.* "Aubade Cassette" will appear in *Dusie Poetry Journal.* "Another World Gathers" and "This is Why I Need a Goddess" will appear in *Four Way Review.*

ABOUT THE AUTHOR

Born in Iloilo City, Philippines, **Angela Peñaredondo** is a poet and artist. She received her MFA from the University of California, Riverside. Her work has appeared or is forthcoming in *The Margins, The Berkeley Review, Southern Humanities Review, Tuesday; An Art Project, South Dakota Review, Thrush Poetry Journal* and elsewhere. She is also a VONA/Voices of Our Nations Art fellow. Angela has a chapbook titled, *Maroon* (Jamii Publishing).

All Things Lose Thousands of Times is her first full-length collection of poetry.

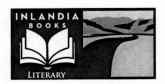

CPSIA information can be obtained
at www.ICGtesting.com
Printed in the USA
LVOW12s2356220816
501369LV00004B/183/P